Hello, Family Members,

Learning to read is one of the most important accomplishments of early childhood. **Hello Reader!** books are designed to help children become skilled readers who like to read. Beginning readers learn to read by remembering frequently used words like "the," "is," and "and"; by using phonics skills to decode new words; and by interpreting picture and text clues. These books provide both the stories children enjoy and the structure they need to read fluently and independently. Here are suggestions for helping your child *before*, *during*, and *after* reading:

Before

- Look at the cover and pictures and have your child predict what the story is about.
- Read the story to your child.
- Encourage your child to chime in with familiar words and phrases.
- Echo read with your child by reading a line first and having your child read it after you do.

During

- Have your child think about a word he or she does not recognize right away. Provide hints such as "Let's see if we know the sounds" and "Have we read other words like this one?"
- Encourage your child to use phonics skills to sound out new words.
- Provide the word for your child when more assistance is needed so that he or she does not struggle and the experience of reading with you is a positive one.
- Encourage your child to have fun by reading with a lot of expression . . . like an actor!

After

- Have your child keep lists of interesting and favorite words.
- Encourage your child to read the books over and over again. Have him or her read to brothers, sisters, grandparents, and even teddy bears. Repeated readings develop confidence in young readers.
- Talk about the stories. Ask and answer questions. Share ideas about the funniest and most interesting characters and events in the stories.

I do hope that you and your child enjoy this book.

—Francie Alexander
Chief Education Officer,
Scholastic's Learning Ventures

To Kaj
— F.R.

To Lula Brockman Estes
— J.C.

Thanks to Russell K. Pearl
of the Chicago Herpetological Society
and Paul Sieswerda
of the New York Aquarium
for their expertise.

Go to scholastic.com for web site information
on Scholastic authors and illustrators.

ISBN: 0-439-33014-9

Text copyright © 2002 by Fay Robinson.
Illustrations copyright © 2002 by Jean Cassels.
All rights reserved. Published by Scholastic Inc.
SCHOLASTIC, HELLO READER!, CARTWHEEL BOOKS, and associated logos
are trademarks and/or registered trademarks of Scholastic Inc.

Library of Congress Cataloging-in-Publication Data

Robinson, Fay.
    Cool Chameleons! / by Fay Robinson ; illustrated by Jean Cassels.
        p. cm. — (Hello reader! Science—Level 2)
    Summary: Describes the physical characteristics and behavior of chameleons.
    ISBN: 0-439-33014-9 (pbk.)
        1. Chameleons—Juvenile literature. [1. Chameleons.] I. Cassels, Jean. II. Title.
    III. Hello science reader! Level 2.

QL666.L23 R63 2002
597.95'6—dc21   2001032265

10 9 8 7 6   05 06

Printed in the U.S.A.   23
First printing, March 2002

Cool Chameleons!

by Fay Robinson
Illustrated by Jean Cassels

Hello Reader! Science—Level 2

SCHOLASTIC INC. Cartwheel ·B·O·O·K·S· ®

New York   Toronto   London   Auckland   Sydney
Mexico City   New Delhi   Hong Kong   Buenos Aires

Little lizards,
tree-top wizards—

very cool chameleons!

Leaf-shaped bodies,
curly tails,

wrinkled skin,
and bead-like scales.

Funny faces,
large and lumpy,

always frowning,
looking grumpy.

Pea-shaped eyes look all around—
one goes up and one goes down.

Slowly climbing
jungle trees—

toes and tails
hold on with ease.

Black and red or blue and green—
every color in between!

Spots and circles,
dark and light—

aren't chameleons quite a sight?

Changing colors when they're mad,
cold or hot,

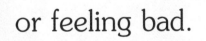

or feeling bad.

Many seem to disappear.
Can you find the
chameleon here?

Eggs are buried in the ground.
Out of sight, they're safe and sound.

Babies hatching—one, two, three.

Babies climbing their first tree.

Time to eat.
Eyes look about.

They spot a bug.
A tongue flies out.

Zap!

The bug gets hit and stuck.

Snap!
The hungry mouth slams shut!

Noses come with

crusty humps,

pointy tips,

or little bumps.

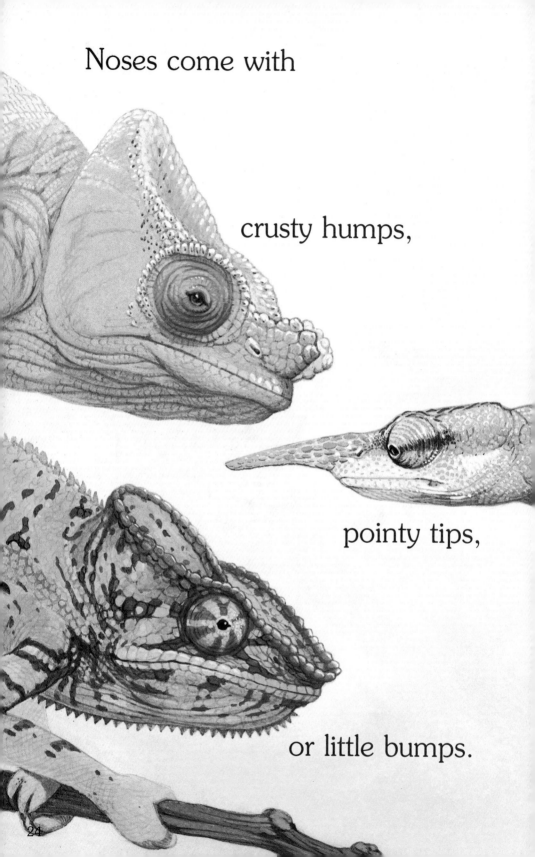

Some may look like
cobs of corn.
Others shine with
long, sharp horns!

Heads with humps

and heads with flaps.

Heads with tall,
green party hats!

Like dragons out of storybooks,
they guard the trees
with frightful looks.

Little lizards,
tree-top wizards—
very cool chameleons!

Cover:
Senegal Chameleon

Page 4:
Panther Chameleon

Page 5:
Jeweled Chameleon

Page 6:
Parson's Chameleon

Page 7:
Spiny Chameleon

Page 7:
Tusked Chameleon

Page 8:
Senegal Chameleon

Page 9:
Carpet Chameleon
(Female)

Page 9:
Carpet Chameleon
(Male)

Page 10:
La Bord's Chameleo

Pages 10 & 11:
Panther Chameleon

Page 11:
Panther Chameleon

Page 12:
Flap-necked
Chameleon

Page 15:
Senegal Chameleon

Page 20:
Panther
Chameleon

Page 12:
Minor's Chameleon
(Female)

Page 16:
Elephant-eared
Chameleon

Page 21:
Panther
Chameleon

Page 13:
Carpet Chameleon

Page 18:
Senegal Chameleon

Page 22:
Panther Chameleon

Page 14:
Senegal Chameleon

Page 19:
Senegal Chameleon

Page 23:
Panther Chameleon

Page 24:
Parson's Chameleon

Page 25:
Jackson's Chameleon

Page 27:
Veiled Chameleon

Page 24:
Long-nosed
Chameleon

Page 26:
Helmeted Chameleon

Page 28:
Mountain Chameleo

Page 24:
Panther Chameleon

Page 25:
Fischer's Chameleon

Page 26:
Elephant-eared
Chameleon

Page 29:
Tusked Chameleon